D1530932

MINI
MYTHS
TALES FROM ANCIENT GREECE

# THE LABORS OF
# HERCULES

Michael DeMocker

PURPLE TOAD
PUBLISHING

P.O. Box 631
Kennett Square, Pennsylvania 19348
www.purpletoadpublishing.com

**PURPLE TOAD**
PUBLISHING

Printing
1    2    3    4    5    6    7    8    9

Fabulous Fables
Heroic Heroes
The Labors of Hercules
Mythical Monsters
Tantalizing Tales

**Publisher's Cataloging-in-Publication Data**
DeMocker, Michael
  The Labors of Hercules / Michael DeMocker
    p. cm.—(Mini myths of Ancient Greece)
Includes bibliographic references and index.
ISBN: 978-1-62469-064-8 (library bound)
1. Mythology, Greek – Juvenile literature.  2. Heracles (Greek Mythology)—Juvenile literature.
I. Title.
  BL820.H5 2013
  398.2093802—dc23
                                                          2013936503

eBook ISBN: 9781624690655

**ABOUT THE AUTHOR:** Despite being a dashingly handsome, globe-trotting, award-winning photojournalist and travel writer based in New Orleans, Michael DeMocker is, in truth, really quite dull, a terrible dancer, and a frequent source of embarrassment to his wife, son and three dogs.

Printed by Lake Book Manufacturing, Chicago, IL

# CONTENTS

Have you ever had to do chores that you hated? I did. I had a list of the twelve most dangerous chores that I had to finish to earn back my freedom. Oh, but I am getting ahead of myself.

I am Hercules, the greatest Greek hero. Songs, statues, and paintings have been made in my honor. Nice, right? But things didn't start out that way. In fact, my life started pretty badly.

You see, my father was the Greek god, Zeus, and my mother was a mortal woman named Alcmene. Hera, Zeus's wife, hated me. It wasn't MY fault! You can't choose your parents! But Hera set out to make my life miserable.

First, she put two deadly snakes in my crib!
WHO PUTS SNAKES IN A BABY'S CRIB? Well,
luckily I am half-god on my father's side, so I
strangled the snakes with my bare baby hands.
But that didn't save me from Hera's wrath.

As I grew, I became stronger and stronger,
but Hera tricked me into taking the lives of my
own family. In order to receive forgiveness for
my crime (which was Hera's fault), I was given
twelve impossible chores by my cowardly
cousin, King Eurystheus.

These chores were called "The Twelve
Labors." A labor is like a chore, only IT CAN
KILL YOU! Of course, no one gets eaten by a
nine-headed monster while taking out the trash!

# The Labors of Hercules
# THE NEMEAN LION

My first labor on the worst list of chores ever made, was to slay the Nemean Lion. No big deal, right? He's just a big cat and I am a powerful hero!

Oh, did I mention that this lion had super skin and could not be hurt by weapons? That it is the offspring of two hideous monsters? So, to defeat it I had to fight the giant beast with my bare hands.

I strangled the lion after a nasty fight in its cave. I used the lion's own claw to skin its body and make myself a cape from its pelt.

# The Labors of Hercules
## THE HYDRA

And did I get a break from monsters? No.

Next, I had to battle a poisonous creature with nine heads called the Hydra.

Any guess as to who created a poisonous nine-headed monster just to kill me? That's right, it was Hera! Worse yet, if one of the Hydra's heads is cut off, then two more grow back in its place!

To stop this beast, the trick is to cut off each head, then use a torch to burn where the heads were so nothing could grow back. Gross, right? But it beats getting eaten!

I was just about to defeat the Hydra when Hera sent a giant crab to attack me.

This was totally unfair, so I stepped on the crab with a mighty crunch. Then I beat the Hydra once and for all.

# THE GOLDEN HIND

Luckily, the third chore on the list was to catch a very fast deer with golden antlers called a hind. This task was a nice break from all the monster fighting.

As easy as it seemed, it took me a year to finally catch the hind. I showed it to Eurystheus, and then I let it go.
I hoped my next labor wouldn't be to fight a terrible monster.

# THE ERYMANTHIAN BOAR

My next labor was to fight another monster—
a giant wild pig called the Erymanthian Boar.
This wasn't too hard for me; I just chased the
boar into heavy snow where it couldn't move and
tied it up. When I brought the bound creature to
Eurystheus to prove I had caught it, he hid in a
giant jar out of fear!

## The Labors of Hercules
# CLEANING THE STABLES

For this labor, I had to do some cleaning. Not so bad, right? I'll bet when you have to clean your room, it isn't as bad as fighting a nine-headed monster, although to be fair I haven't seen your room. It turns out what I had to clean was a stable filled with one thousand magic cattle—and the stable had not been cleaned in 30 years. I don't mean to be gross, but do you have any idea how much dung there was? AND I HAD ONLY ONE DAY TO CLEAN IT! Well, I had the great idea to use my super strength to divert two near-by rivers to . . . no giggling here . . . flush it all away. STOP GIGGLING! THIS WAS A GROSS LABOR!

Fine, giggle all you want.

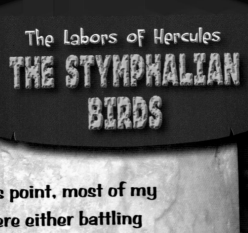

# THE STYMPHALIAN BIRDS

Up to this point, most of my labors were either battling monsters or battling cow dung. For the sixth, I got BOTH! My labor was to chase away the Stymphalian birds, man-eaters with, you guessed it, poisonous poop! But, using a noise-making rattle, I scared the birds into the air and shot so many of them with a bow and arrow, the rest flew away in fear.

# THE CRETAN BULL

**HALFWAY THERE!** I was starting to feel pretty good about finishing my list and being freed. Next, I sailed to the island of Crete where there was trouble with the king's pet bull. Only this was no ordinary bull. It was ferocious and mean, and, no joking, it could walk on water. I sneaked up on the bull and wrestled it to the ground. I then rode on its back all the way from Crete back home again. Can you imagine what the sailors thought when they saw me riding a bull past their ships?

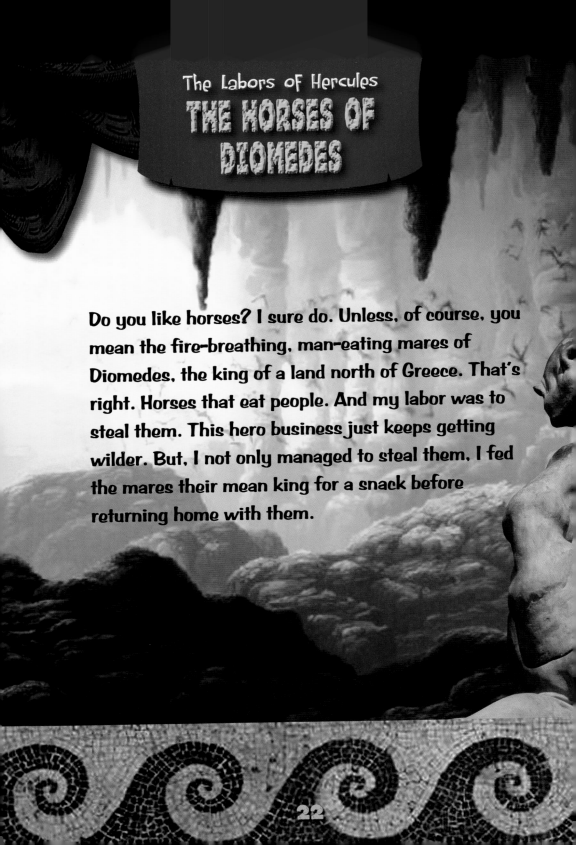

# THE HORSES OF DIOMEDES

Do you like horses? I sure do. Unless, of course, you mean the fire-breathing, man-eating mares of Diomedes, the king of a land north of Greece. That's right. Horses that eat people. And my labor was to steal them. This hero business just keeps getting wilder. But, I not only managed to steal them, I fed the mares their mean king for a snack before returning home with them.

# THE BELT OF HIPPOLYTA

Have you noticed something about the last few labors? No Hera! Maybe she would finally leave me alone to finish them. Yeah right! My next task was to get the belt of Hippolyta, queen of the Amazons.

I used my heroic handsomeness and tales of my adventures to convince the queen to give me her belt. However, before she could, Hera, disguised as an Amazon, tricked the other Amazon warriors into attacking me! I had no choice but to kill Hippolyta and take the belt. There is only Hera to blame.

# The Labors of Hercules
## THE CATTLE OF GERYON

Next, I had to travel to the island of Erytheia to steal some cows. I can hear you now! What kind of cows, Hercules, ten-horned, poisonous monster cows that have the teeth of a shark? No! Not at all! These were just regular cows. I thought I'd finally caught a break.

But, no, it turns out they were guarded by a two-headed monster dog named Orthrus and his giant, three-headed monster owner Geryon. I bonked the dog with my club and killed Geryon with an arrow dipped in the Hydra's poison, then herded the cows away.

# THE GOLDEN APPLES

OK, please please let me have a labor with no monsters. So, the next labor is to fetch some golden apples in the far off garden of the Hesperides. The apples allow you to live forever and are tended by seven happy nymphs. Nymphs with fruit! Sounds totally safe, you say! Were you paying attention to the ten previous labors?

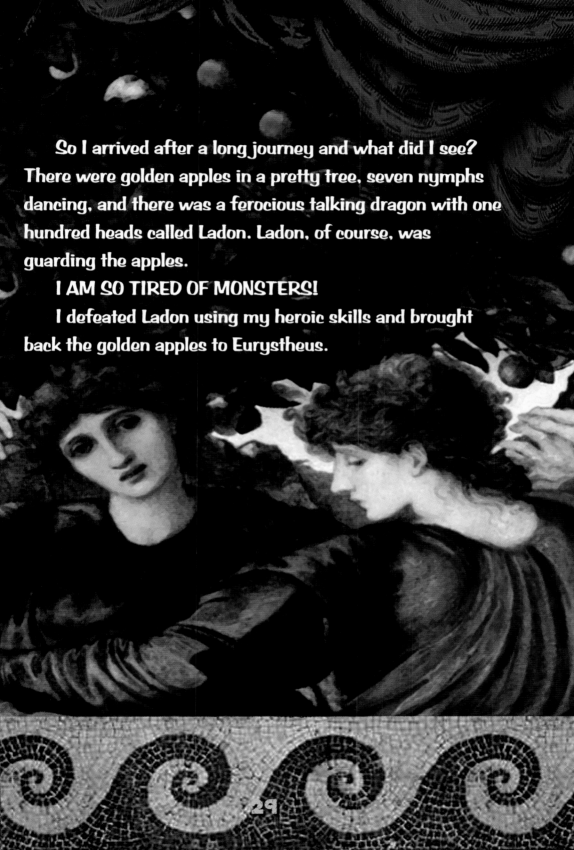

So I arrived after a long journey and what did I see? There were golden apples in a pretty tree, seven nymphs dancing, and there was a ferocious talking dragon with one hundred heads called Ladon. Ladon, of course, was guarding the apples.

I AM SO TIRED OF MONSTERS!

I defeated Ladon using my heroic skills and brought back the golden apples to Eurystheus.

**THE LAST LABOR!** And guess what, I didn't have to kill a monster! No, I just had to catch a dog. I love dogs! Only this dog had a snake for a tail and three heads.

And he belonged to Hades, god of the Underworld where the dead reside.

The dog was Cerberus and he was a dog that would rather eat your house than fetch your slippers. Good news though! Hades said I could take him. All I had to do was defeat the dog. So Cereberus and I battled each other in a long round of wrestling. Luckily, I won.

I returned to King Eurystheus and showed him Cerberus.

I had finally finished my labors and was free! I took Cerberus back to his home and started my new life.

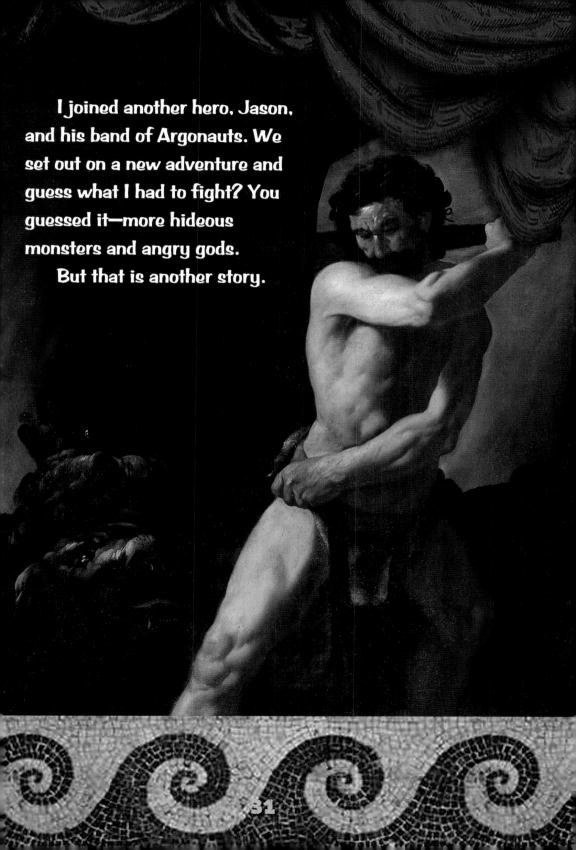

I joined another hero, Jason, and his band of Argonauts. We set out on a new adventure and guess what I had to fight? You guessed it—more hideous monsters and angry gods.

But that is another story.

# FURTHER READING

## Books

Harris, John. *Greece! Rome! Monsters!* Los Angeles, California: Getty Publications, 2002

McCaughrean, Geraldine. *Greek Gods and Goddesses*. New York: Margaret K. McElderry Books, 1998

Oh, Cirro. *Greek and Roman Mythology, Volumes 1, 2, & 3*. Singapore: Youngjin Singapore Pte, Ltd., 2005.

## Works Consulted

Bulfinch, Thomas. *Bulfinch's Mythology: The Age of Fable*. Mineola, New York: Dover Publications, 2000.

Green, Roger Lancelyn. *Tales of Greek Heroes*. London: Penguin Books, 1958, 2002.

Hamilton, Edith. *Mythology*. New York: Warner Books, 1999.

McLean, Mollie, and Anne Wiseman. *Adventures of Greek Heroes*. New York: Houghton Mifflin, 1961, 1989.

Rouse, W.H.D. *Gods, Heroes and Men of Ancient Greece*. New York: New American Library, 1957, 2001.

## On the Internet

Ancient Greece: Hercules
http://www.ducksters.com/history/ancient_greece/hercules.php

*History Channel*: Greek Gods
http://www.history.com/topics/hercules/videos

The Labors of Hercules
http://www.perseus.tufts.edu/Herakles/labors.html

# INDEX